CODEPENDENCY

CODEPENDENCY

PAT SPRINGLE

Rapha Publishing/Word, Inc.

Houston and Dallas, TX

Codependency
by Pat Springle
© 1991 by Rapha, Inc.

Second Printing, 1992
ISBN: 0-945276-26-5
Printed in the United States of America

CONTENTS

FAMILY SYSTEMS OF BEHAVIOR

Significant research has contributed to much of what we know about family systems of behavior.[1] For purposes of simplification, these systems are identified as the functional family and the dysfunctional family.

The functional family, or family which contributes to the overall growth and development of its members, certainly isn't perfect. It does, however, foster open, honest, loving communication. In this environment, both the parents and their children develop a strong sense of "self," or identity. They learn

1

that they can trust, feel, and talk about many—
if not all—the issues in their lives.

When parents are healthy and their home
environment is characterized by love, children
are able to develop positive self-concepts.
They are able to have positive, productive
roles in society and meet life's challenges
adequately.

In a dysfunctional family system, open,
honest, loving communication is thwarted.
Family dysfunction may be characterized by
chemical dependency, workaholism, divorce,
eating or sexual disorders, an emotionally and/
or physically absent parent, neglect, abuse
(verbal, emotional, physical, sexual), a
domineering and/or passive parent, gambling
or excessive spending, a family member who
is handicapped, physically or mentally ill, or
who manifests some other type of disorder.
Resulting problems in family interaction may
cause members to feel that something is
wrong, but negative communication systems
hinder the freedom and ability to be honest

about their feelings. Denial, an unwillingness or inability to recognize problems in and around one's "self," promotes more repression and further erodes family trust and intimacy. The result is that the family unit to some degree lacks the love, worth, stability, and discipline its members need.

In the dysfunctional family system, the primary goal of family members is survival. Very little development takes place in the children. In fact, most normal self-development is lost. All of the unconscious focus is on the primary dysfunctional person. Children in these systems rarely build healthy self-concepts. They are at great risk for multiple marriages, addiction, codependency, and stress-related physical problems.

Our Needs to Be Loved and Feel Valued

All people are created with a God-given need to be loved and to have a sense of worth. It is God's intent that these needs be met by two primary sources: the grace of God through

3

Christ and the reflection of His grace and strength in the family. These two sources are not meant to function separately, but are intended to form a cohesive environment. The content of the Gospel will have fertile soil when parents model God's character to their children.

It is difficult to overestimate the family's influence in a person's development. A child can grow up in a home where the parents are Christians, but are too strict, critical, or neglectful (all types of dysfunctional attributes can exist in Christian families). The result will be a hurting, guilt-ridden, driven, overly responsible, or completely passive person; that is, a codependent. On the other hand, a child can be nurtured and protected in a home where the parents aren't believers. The warmth, affection, attention, and strength in this family will be much more likely to produce a stable and secure child than in a codependent, Christian household. This may sound like heresy to some people, but children don't care a lot about theology. They care about being loved—really loved, not just in words but in deeds—with time, attention, and affection. They need time to relax, study, and play together, to be listened to and comforted when they hurt, and praised when they do well. Parents can do that. Empty theology can't.

When a person lives in an environment of love and acceptance, he tends to blossom. In dysfunctional families, where these basic needs aren't met, people are left to find other avenues to meet those pressing needs. The compelling goal of their lives becomes having those needs met. Everything they say or do is consciously or unconsciously designed to numb their pain and gain a sense of intimacy with others and a sense of worth in their own eyes. Some escape to passivity. Some are driven to succeed to prove their worth. Most of us do both in varying combinations.

Some aspects of codependency are pitiful. Codependency crushes a person. It crushes his stability and his identity. It keeps him from enjoying all that God has for him. According to some psychiatrists and psychologists, the crushing nature of codependency does its awful work in the majority of people when they are most vulnerable: while they are young children. The eminent Harvard physician and child psychiatrist, Dr. Burton White, has found that in the first three years of a child's life, the home environment is critical. Dr. White does not take into account the power of God's Spirit to change lives, but his point is well taken: it is extremely difficult for a child to change his self-concept after the age of three![2]

Codependents long to be loved. They desperately want to have a sense of worth and specialness. Those needs are God-given, but in a codependent family, the resources to meet those needs have often been withheld.

The Cause of Codependency

Perhaps a chart will help explain both the cause and the effects of codependency. In the following chart, the God-given needs for love, security, worth, protection, and provision are presented first. Then, two possible environments are listed: one for a functional family and one for a dysfunctional family, with corresponding effects or consequences of each. The chart concludes with the motivational patterns that healthy and codependent people develop.

Too often, we look at the behavior and emotions of codependency—either in ourselves or other people—and try to "fix" them without examining their cause. Hopefully, this chart will help you see that there is a very clear cause.

Needs	Environment	Results	Motivation
Love Security Worth	**Functional family:** love, acceptance, forgiveness, protection, provision, honesty, freedom to feel, loving discipline	**Spiritual, emotional, relational health:** love, anger, fear, laughter, intimacy, willingness to take risks	**Healthy motives:** love, thankfulness, obedience out of gratitude
Protection Provisions	**Dysfunctional family:** (alchoholism, drug abuse, eating disorders, etc.): condemnation, manipulation, neglect, abuse, unreality, denial	**Codependency:** lack of objectivity, warped sense of responsibility, controlled/ controlling, guilt, hurt and anger, loneliness	**Compulsive motives:** avoid pain, fear of rejection, fear of failure, gain a sense of worth, accomplish goals to win approval

Examples of Codependent Behavior

Before we attempt to define codependency and explore whether or not our lives may be governed by codependent characteristics, let's look at some examples of codependent behavior.

Scott is from a small Midwestern town where his father is a prominent lawyer and his mother is a high school chemistry teacher. He has two brothers and two sisters, all four of whom are considerably older than he is.

His father is a highly respected member of the community, but when he comes home, this model citizen becomes a bear. He is often verbally abusive and loud. Scott's brothers and sisters helped each other grow up in that environment, but they didn't help Scott. He was the kid brother; the "odd man out." His mother didn't help either. Even when Scott was taking a terrible tongue-lashing from his father, his mother would look the other way— and get a drink. Her method of coping with the anger in their family was found in pints, fifths, and quarts.

His two brothers took a cue from their father and began to pick on Scott when he was in junior high school. But they went beyond verbal abuse. They beat him and pushed him around. He felt alone—very much alone.

Though he was bright, witty, and a good athlete, Scott could never do enough to please his parents. He looked for ways to help them and make them proud of him, but instead of winning their approval, he was always criticized for not doing better.

As Scott and I talked about his family, I asked him if he had any particularly painful memories. He recalled several specific incidents of his father screaming at him for normal childhood mistakes like spilling milk or not doing so well on a test in school. He also remembered his mother leaving him alone to sort through his father's wrath—no comfort from her! He remembered a particularly bad beating he got from his oldest brother one day after school. And then he remembered the bicycle.

Scott's father always bought each of his children a new bike on their twelfth birthday. By the time the fourth sibling had turned twelve, there were four nice bikes lined up in the garage, and Scott knew his turn was coming. As his twelfth birthday approached, he could hardly wait to get his bike. He had stopped at the bike shop almost every day for weeks, and he had just the right one picked out!

On his birthday, Scott hurried down to breakfast and found a box on the breakfast table. It felt too heavy for just a card that would promise him a new bike that afternoon. He tore open the box and found a football. He looked at his father with an expression of anxiety mixed with fading hope. Was the football in addition to the bike? His father snorted, "I hope you like the ball."

"But...what about my bike, Dad?"

"Is that the thanks I get for giving you a birthday present?" He snarled. "Besides, I couldn't afford to get you a bike. I just bought a new boat yesterday. It'll be here tomorrow."

The boat sat in the garage for years. Scott's father rarely used it. Every time Scott walked into the garage and saw the four bicycles and that boat, he had to look the other way. It hurt too much to think about.

Today, Scott still tries to control his parents' attitudes by doing whatever they ask him to do. He tries to fix, rescue, and help, but he thinks of himself as a failure no matter how well he does. He is plagued by nightmares, and he has difficulty controlling his thoughts. Though he is a tenderhearted and perceptive man, he has very few, if any, deep friendships. He feels very lonely.

When Richard started dating Betty, he could tell that she was a girl who knew how to have a good time! She was the life of the party. Sometimes she drank a little too much, but he'd say, "That's just Betty. She'll be all right." After they got married, life sailed along for a while, but Betty's drinking began to be a problem. She started drinking martinis at lunch and a couple of margaritas after work. "It helps me relax," she explained.

When she felt bad and didn't get the house cleaned up, Richard did it for her. When she was hung over and couldn't go to work, she asked Richard to call and tell her boss that she was sick. The first few times this happened, Richard did these things with the rationale that it surely wouldn't happen again. But it did.

Betty's drinking got progressively worse, and Richard was giving excuses to friends, neighbors, bosses, and everyone else they knew to cover for her irresponsibility. He not only worked hard at his job, he also worked hard at home. He washed clothes, cleaned, cooked, and he made excuses for Betty.

Richard wanted to have children, and thought, *Maybe a child will help Betty; maybe she will stop drinking and be okay*. Ashley was born after they had been married for five years, but instead of helping Betty to stop drinking and become more responsible, Richard was expected to do more. He had to be both a mother and a father to Ashley. He loved his wife and child, but he became tired and angered by their demands. Then he felt guilty for being angry with his little girl. Richard's life was a wreck!

When they were first married, Richard had rationalized Betty's problem, and had felt compassion for her. But now he was angry. He felt used and lonely, and yet he continued to help Betty and make excuses for her. And he felt sorry for himself; sorry that anyone as kind and thoughtful as he was could be so misunderstood and mistreated. He even thought about taking Ashley and leaving Betty, but he wondered, *Where would she go to find somebody like me to take care of her? What would she do without me? She needs me!* So Richard stayed. He continued to "rescue" Betty, he continued to be angry with her, and he continued to feel sorry for himself. Nothing changed. Ever.

Gwen's father was a successful businessman and a deacon in the church. Everybody in town felt that he was a model citizen and father, but he ran his home like a business, too. He was strict and demanding, rarely showing any affection to Gwen and her brother.

When she was seven years old, Gwen's uncle, Frank, came to stay while her parents were out of town for two weeks. One night, as she was getting ready for bed, Frank walked into Gwen's room and began hugging her. He said, "Gwen, I've always loved you so much. You're so special to me." Then he began touching her in places that just didn't seem right to her. Gwen was startled, surprised, and confused. She was starved for affection, but this kind of affection left her feeling dirty. Frank then told her, "Now, let's keep this a secret between you and me. It would spoil it if your parents knew, and I would be very angry if you told them."

Over the next several years, Frank offered to stay with Gwen and her brother as often as possible. Each time, the same things happened: the fondling, the tenderness, the secrecy, and the threats. Gwen dreaded hearing Frank's voice.

Gwen grew up being condemned by her father and molested by her uncle, and she had no one to talk to. Her initial confusion turned to self-condemnation, and her self-condemnation to self-hatred. She saw herself as dirty, obscene, and revolting.

When she was 20, Gwen became a Christian. She knew she needed forgiveness, but even after she had trusted Christ, she continued to feel confused and withdrawn. The other Christians she knew seemed to be so happy, and they seemed to be learning so much. In the midst of their enthusiasm, Gwen became all the more withdrawn, despising herself even more.

Defining Codependency

Originally, *codependent* was applied to family members of alcoholics. Later, the term was given to families of those who were dependent on any kind of drug, including alcohol. Today the word is used to describe anyone in a significant relationship with a person who exhibits any kind of dependency. Some dependencies are more subtle than others, and in addition to alcohol and drugs, may include sex, food, work, perfectionism, success, spending, another person, etc. Codependents are those who are adversely affected by the dependent person's behavior and who have an imbalanced sense of responsibility to rescue, fix, and/or help the dependent person. The dependent person either consciously or unconsciously deprives the codependent of needed love and affirmation. This provokes rescuing as a means of obtaining that affirmation.

Everybody, it seems, has his own definition of codependency. Here are some examples:

- Codependency is bondage to pleasing somebody.
- It is being controlled by someone and trying to control him.
- It is being dependent on making someone else happy.
- Codependency is the responsibility to make others happy, successful, and good.
- It is a hurting child in an adult's body.

- It is feeling guilty when you don't do everything just right—and that's all the time!
- Codependency is trying to make a sick person well and making yourself sick!

In her best-selling book, *Codependent No More*, Melody Beattie defines a codependent person as "one who has let another person's behavior affect him or her, and who is obsessed with controlling that person's behavior."[3]

We will define codependency as *a compulsion to control and rescue people by fixing their problems.* It occurs when a person's God-given needs for love and security have been blocked in a relationship with a dysfunctional person, resulting in a lack of objectivity, a warped sense of responsibility (three primary characteristics); and in hurt and anger, guilt and loneliness (three corollary characteristics). These characteristics affect the codependent's every

18

relationship and desire. His life goal is to avoid the pain of being unloved and to find ways to prove that he is lovable. In his desire to please others, he loses his identity. He takes on the feelings of others as his own. And he tries to act in ways that will suit other people. If he does have the courage to feel, think, and act differently, he usually is defensive when confronted, and feels guilty for pursuing his own identity.

This is not to suggest, as some assert, that almost any relational problem or desire to please people is a sign of codependency. The problem is more specific than that. Codependency is a compulsion to rescue others, a sense of having to get the approval of others at all costs, and a need to control the emotions, attitudes, and behaviors of others.

The important point is not how narrowly or broadly we define codependency, but to understand why we feel, think, and act as we do so that we can begin to experience healthy change. For our purposes, we will define codependency narrowly and apply it broadly.

As codependents, we...
- feel responsible for others' behavior, but often don't take responsibility for our own.
- need to be needed.
- expect others to make us happy.
- can be demanding or indecisive.
- can be attentive and caring or selfish and cruel.
- often see people and situations as wonderful or awful, "black or white," with no room for ambiguity, or "gray."
- often overreact to people or situations which we can't control.
- seek affirmation and attention, or sulk and hide.
- believe we are perceptive, and sometimes are, but often can't see reality in our own lives.
- see others as being "for us" or "against us."
- get hurt easily.

- use self-pity and/or anger to manipulate others.
- feel like we need to rescue people from themselves.
- communicate contrasting messages, like, *I need you. I hate you.*
- are deeply repentant, but commit the same sins again and again.

We can change! Our lives can be different! We can experience freedom from the compulsion to rescue and control others. We can learn to develop deep, healthy relationships. First, however, we must understand why we feel and act as we do. Understanding is the foundation of hope for change. With understanding and hope, we then can begin (or continue) a process toward spiritual, emotional, and relational health.

CHARACTERISTICS OF CODEPENDENCY

In order to gain a better understanding of the unhealthy relational patterns that comprise codependent behavior, let's look at the most common characteristics of codependency.

Primary Characteristics

A Lack of Objectivity - Despite the highly perceptive nature of most codependents, members of dysfunctional families usually believe that their family is "normal." They simply cannot see the unhealthy ways in which their family relates to one another because they never have experienced emotionally healthy relationships. Also, coming to grips with the pain, hurt, anger, and manipulation they've suffered can be very threatening. Solving other people's crises absorbs so much of the codependent's energy that the prospect of any more pain or anger simply is too much to bear. For this reason, codependents tend to deny the existence of most problems and their unhealthy patterns of relating continue.

A Warped Sense of Responsibility - Common synonyms for codependency are: rescue, help, fix, and enable. The codependent sees himself as a savior; he is driven to help others, especially the emotionally sick and addicted people in his or her family. The addict (or dysfunctional person) is unwilling or unable to take care of himself, so he may use both self-pity and condemnation to evoke a helping response from the overly-responsible codependent. The codependent wants to be loved and accepted, and wants to avoid conflict, so he does whatever it takes to make the dependent person happy. The codependent is so busy taking care of others, however, that he neglects to care of himself by making his own decisions and determining his own identity and behavior.

Controlled and Controlling - Like everyone else, codependents need love and respect, but having been deprived of these precious commodities, they determine to do whatever it takes to win the affirmation they crave. Their means to that end is to make people happy. Their chief fear is that people will be unhappy with them. Those around the codependent quickly learn how to use motivators such as praise and condemnation, as well as guilt and comparison, to manipulate him as artfully as a puppeteer maneuvers a puppet.

Modeling is a powerful teacher; codependents typically treat others as they have been treated.

Corollary Characteristics

Hurt and Anger - Addiction creates a family system of communication that may include words of love and acceptance, but the actions demonstrated by family members often hurt deeply.

Physical and verbal abuse obviously leave the codependent feeling deeply hurt and angered by the ones who have inflicted pain upon him. But the passive abuse of neglect and withdrawal are equally devastating. The family that is supposed to provide an atmosphere of warmth and worth instead provides pain. The codependent then attempts to please and rescue the one(s) hurting him in order to win the love he so desperately needs. Although he may be temporarily rewarded for his attempts to please, his needs for unconditional love will remain unmet and his hurt will continue to grow.

Hurt and anger go hand-in-glove. Hurt results from feeling abandoned, used, and condemned, rather than loved and valued. Anger is a reaction toward the source of the hurt.

Guilt - Codependents often feel guilty. They feel guilty for what they've done and haven't done, for what they've said, haven't said, felt and haven't felt. They feel guilty for just about everything. Often such guilt produces feelings of worthlessness and shame.

The codependent gets his worth—his identity—from what he does for others. He rescues, he helps, he enables, but no matter how much he does for others, it's never enough. That's the trap of living in a dysfunctional family: he rescues but is rejected. Lacking objectivity, he concludes, *It's my fault. If I were a better person, they would love me.* He spends his life trying to be good enough to earn the love and acceptance he so desperately wants but fears he never will have. And he's haunted by the shame of feeling that he hasn't—or can't— measure up.

Loneliness - Codependents spend their lives giving, helping, and serving others. They may appear to be the most social people in the world, but inside they are lonely. Their attempts to please others by helping and serving are designed to win affection. Though they may occasionally see a glimpse of love and respect, it usually fades all too quickly. Then, thinking they have been abandoned by both people and God, they feel empty and companionless. They distrust authority, believing that anyone above them is against them, and they build elaborate facades to hide their painful feelings of loneliness.

All of us experience these characteristics to some degree, but a codependent's life is characterized by them.

Are You Codependent?*

1. Do you often feel isolated and afraid of people, especially authority figures?

2. Have you observed yourself to be an approval-seeker, losing your own identity in the process?

3. Do you feel overly frightened of angry people and personal criticism?

4. Do you often feel you are a victim in personal and career relationships?

5. Do you sometimes feel you have an overdeveloped sense of responsibility, which makes it easier to be more concerned with others than with yourself?

6. Is it hard for you to look at your own faults and be responsible for yourself?

7. Do you feel guilty when you stand up for yourself instead of giving in to others?

8. Do you feel addicted to excitement?

9. Do you confuse love with pity, and tend to love people you can pity and rescue?

*Adapted from an ACOA questionnaire.

10. Is it hard for you to experience or express feelings, including feelings like joy or happiness?
11. Do you judge yourself harshly?
12. Do you have a low sense of self-esteem?
13. Do you often feel abandoned in the course of your relationships?
14. Do you tend to be a reactor instead of an initiator?

If you answered yes to two of these questions, you have codependent tendencies.

If you answered yes to four of these questions, you probably are codependent.

If you answered yes to six or more, you are codependent.

Some have asked, "Aren't all people codependent?" No, they aren't. All people have experienced the effects of sin and, to a degree, share the misery of codependent characteristics, but codependents experience these difficulties at a much deeper level.

Are we saying that codependents are terrible people? Certainly not! Codependents are some of the most generous, sensitive, bright, articulate, efficient, effective, and wonderful people on earth. But they are hurting, lonely people who desperately want to be loved. Consequently, they try to fix people and things. They try to make others happy without thinking of their own happiness, allowing themselves to be controlled by the praise and condemnation of others, while also trying to control their own lives. Codependents give up their own identity, their own ideas, and their own emotions and force themselves instead to feel and act in a way that pleases other people. Why? Because they so desperately want to be loved. Ultimately, these coping behaviors don't work. No matter how hard they try (and some try so hard that they have emotional and/or physical breakdowns, while others give up and escape into their own world of self-indulgence), their needs for love, worth, and significance go unmet.

THE CODEPENDENT CHRISTIAN

The Gospel of Jesus Christ is a message of freedom, forgiveness, hope, love, joy, and strength. It is the Good News, the most liberating and energizing power mankind has ever, or will ever hear! Through the distorted glasses of codependency, however, this phenomenal message is often seen as oppressive, condemning, and guilt-inducing. Freedom is turned to bondage, forgiveness to guilt, hope to despair, love to condemnation, joy to pessimism, and divine strength to self-sufficiency.

But why? Why is it so difficult for the codependent Christian to understand and apply God's grace?

Ought's and Should's

As we have seen, codependents have a warped sense of responsibility. Since they perceive that their worth comes from their ability to perform, they are driven either to achieve as much as possible or to withdraw in hopelessness. But how does a person measure his performance so he can see if he has achieved value and worth? By doing what he *should* do. By doing what he *ought* to do, and by dividing life into distinct categories: the "have-to's" and the "can't's." This black-and-white definition steals the fun and spontaneity from life and leaves a person with an overactive conscience; pride if he has done well, despair if he hasn't, and a fear of failure and rejection no matter how well he has done. The codependent who is a Christian carries not only society's ought's and should's, he also adds the ought's and should's of Christianity to his already oppressive load. He divorces grace—the source of perspective and power—from the high moral and ethical expectations of the Bible. He then feels obliged to meet these higher expectations, but has only guilt motivation and his own will to achieve them. And the more he reads the Bible, the clearer these expectations and others become, increasing his sense of guilt.

There are many commands in the Scriptures that the codependent Christian misinterprets and applies in his savior mode to gain a sense of worth. Some of these include:

- going the second mile to help someone.
- turning the other cheek when someone hurts him.
- loving those who don't love him.
- giving cheerfully.
- denying his own desires for the sake of others.

- loving his neighbor as he loves himself.
- having a disciplined life of prayer and Bible study.
- letting no unwholesome word proceed from his mouth.
- forgiving, loving, and accepting others as Christ does.
- generally speaking, the worse a person treats him, the more he joyfully serves him.

The codependent Christian believes that he is expected to perform these commands (and all the others) perfectly, with feelings of love, peace, and joy at all times. In the Christian life, he surmises, there is absolutely no room for hurt and anger.

His plight is further complicated by this denial of emotions. His hurt and anger are stuffed away with reasoning like: *A good Christian shouldn't feel this way...so I won't. It's so wonderful to be a Christian...(but I'm dying inside).*

Sooner or later, despair will catch up with him, and his thoughts will become something like this:

If I were walking with God, I wouldn't have these problems.
God has deserted me.
Nobody cares about me. I'm all alone.
Maybe I'm not really a Christian after all.
Surely nobody who feels this way can be a Christian.

But at the same time, he will often defend God so that no one will think badly of Him. Just as the codependent denies his hurt and anger, and excuses and defends the person in his life who has hurt him, he also tries to deny the hurt and anger he perceives that God has caused. And he tries to make sure that God doesn't get any blame for his calamity. In the codependent's eyes, the Savior needs a savior.

Superficial Solutions

Lacking objectivity and being performance-oriented, we look for quick, simple solutions to fix ourselves and other people. There's only one problem—they don't work! Codependency does not lend itself to quick, simple solutions precisely because it is a deep, long-term problem, and not primarily one of wrong action. That could be corrected relatively easily. Ours is a problem of perception.

Real answers are needed that speak to the real issues of worth and identity. These solutions should be experienced in a long process so they will sink in deeply and profoundly. We now will explore our identity in Christ and the profound impact of healthy relationships in the healing process. We also will learn how to identify codependent behavior, how to detach to gain objectivity, and how to make good, healthy decisions.

The Process of Change

The changes that need to occur in a codependent's life (changes in his perceptions of God, of others, of himself, and his lifestyle), require a blend of four components: cognitive, relational, mystical, and temporal, or time. We need to know the truth about God, others, ourselves, and the cognitive aspect. This truth needs to be modeled to us by others, and we need them to encourage, affirm, and correct us, the relational part. But even this is not enough. We need the Lord to work in our lives to give us wisdom, to give us courage to take steps of faith, and to give us power to fight the uphill battle of codependency. And finally, we need time. We live in a society marked by speed, with automated tellers and drive-through banking, fast food, fast sex, telecommunications, microwaves, and more. But years of believing certain things about yourself, God, and others are not changed in an instant! It takes time. Most of us, however, are very impatient. We want change. We want it to be complete. And we want it NOW!

It is counterproductive to expect too much too soon. That usually leads to discouragement and even abandoning the process. Hang in there. The process may be long, and it will be full of ups and downs, but there is hope for change. Now, after that warning, let's examine our identity and sense of worth.

A Biblical Identity

If someone asked, "Who are you?" how would you answer? We usually think of our identity in terms of our function in society. We say, "I'm a salesman." "I'm a mother of three boys." "I'm a lawyer." ...a student ...a secretary. Or maybe we would say, "I'm an American"...a Republican ...a Democrat ...a Christian.

When the apostle John wanted to identify himself in his gospel, he did so relationally. He referred to himself as the disciple whom Jesus loved (John 13:23; 21:7, 20). John's sense of being loved and accepted by Christ was so strong that this was how he identified himself.

When the apostle Paul wrote to the churches, he strongly emphasized teaching the believers about their identities in Christ. His circular letter to the believers in Ephesus is particularly instructive. The first three chapters clearly explain our identities in Christ. Note that even in the first chapter, he uses several key words which relate to our identities: chosen by God (vs. four); adopted by God (vs. five); forgiven by Him (vs. seven); sealed by the Holy Spirit (vs. 13).

There are many other passages about our identity in Christ, but we will not go into them all. Perhaps this chart will give a little more insight into the truth of our identity in Christ. On the left is a list of some characteristics of people who haven't trusted Christ. On the right are some traits of those who have trusted in Christ. The transition is succinctly stated in Col. 1:13-14:

> *For He delivered us from the domain of darkness, and transferred us to the kingdom of His beloved Son,*
>
> *in whom we have redemption, the forgiveness of sins.*

Learning About God's Character

In our book, *Your Parents and You*, Robert McGee, Jim Craddock, and I explain that a person's view of God is shaped by his relationship with his parents. In codependent, dysfunctional families, the children grow up with a distorted view of God. If their parents were (or are) abusive, they will probably believe that God is harsh and condemning. If their parents are neglectful, they will probably believe that God doesn't care about them. Similarly, spouses of compulsive persons can have their view of God adversely affected by that relationship.[4]

The writers of the Scriptures went to great lengths to teach about the character of God, our identity, how we relate to others, and our motivations for obedience. In *The Search for Significance*, Robert McGee outlines several of these motivations in the Scriptures, which include:[5]

- The love of Christ motivates us to obey.
- Sin is destructive.
- The Father will discipline us in love.
- His commands for us are good.
- We will receive rewards.
- Obedience is our opportunity to honor God.

As you can see, guilt is not one of these motivations! Neither is the desire to be accepted! Nor the fear of punishment! There are many good motives found in the Bible, but they are centered on a right view of God and a proper view of our identity as His beloved children. This results in "want-to," not "have-to" motivations.

If you are a codependent, you may have concluded that the commands of Scripture are wrong and harmful. As you begin (or continue) the process of changing your view of God and of the Scriptures, you will see that God is not like the harsh, manipulative, or neglectful person in your life. Nor are you a terrible, worthless person who always has to be more, do more, and say more to be accepted. Yes, you are a sinner, but you are a sinner who has been redeemed by Christ, adopted as a dearly beloved child of God, and given the incredible privilege of knowing, loving, and serving Him.

God loves you! He has demonstrated that love by sending His only Son, Jesus Christ, to pay for your sins so that you can have a relationship with Him now and throughout eternity. Perhaps you have considered Jesus as a good man, or have gone to church, but have never entered into an active relationship with God through the provision of His Son. Take some time to reflect on the verses presented in this booklet. Then, if you want to, express your desire to the Lord to have your sins forgiven and to begin a relationship with Him. You can use your own words, or you can pray something like this:

Lord Jesus, I need You. Thank You for dying on the cross to pay for my sins. I want to receive You as my Savior and Lord. Thank You for forgiving me and giving me eternal life. I want to know You better and experience Your love and grace. Make me the kind of person You want me to be.

The moment that you place your faith in Christ, you will have a new identity based on what Scripture says is true of you! You will be adopted, forgiven, sealed, and secure! Reflect on His work, and trust Him to change your view of yourself, Him, and others.

Applying the Truth of God's Word

For many of us, the truth of who we are in Christ is not new. We have known it for years. We can quote passage after passage, but the Scriptures haven't penetrated past our denial-ridden, codependent Christian facade. We need a fresh look, perhaps through honest people who are struggling with real issues, and who are more interested in real solutions than easy answers. We may not need to change our beliefs about our identity, but we may need to change the depth to which we apply these truths.

The application of these truths in a relationship of love and affirmation is like light and salt to codependents. In this context, we learn to face the truth about ourselves, God, and others. We learn that we have only limited responsibility in the lives of others. It isn't up to us to make people happy. We learn to have our own desires and dreams, and we learn to let other people make their own decisions. We learn to be honest about our emotions: our pain of rejection, intense anger, and disappointments as well as our love and hope. We learn that it's okay to fail because our sense of worth is not threatened by failure, and we learn to try for the right reasons. And finally, we learn to love and be loved, to be honest with people and to give and receive in relationships.

But remember, this doesn't happen all at once. It's like peeling an onion. Each layer brings new revelations, new fears, new hopes and new changes in our lives. Often, we find ourselves dealing repeatedly with the same issues, but it is often at a deeper level or layer. You may be discouraged that there are so many layers! But take heart. Be glad you are in the process of healing. That process, with all of its joys and pains, is a sign of progress.

Author's note: The scope of this booklet does not enable us to go into greater depth about our identity and the character of God. More study and more insights would be very helpful; therefore, I recommend two books with corresponding workbooks to aid your study: *The Search for Significance* and *Your Parents and You.*

Find a Friend

You cannot overcome the grip of codependency alone. You may learn some good information. You may be able to apply some of what you learn at a certain level of your life, but there is too much deception and too little objectivity within us to fight the battle alone. Our thought patterns are too ingrained and our habits too well established. We need the honesty and encouragement of someone else to make substantial progress. We need to see someone model what it means to gain our self-worth from the Lord and experience the freedom and motivation of the Christian life.

This kind of friendship is rare, but there are people (some of whom you may not yet know) who can provide this environment for your growth. Do not look for another codependent who needs you to need him!

48

Don't look for someone to rescue you! Instead, look for someone who will affirm you, encourage you, be honest with you, and be a good model for you.

You may already know someone who can help you, or it may take some looking. A pastor can probably help you find someone, or he may direct you to a group that discusses codependency and emotional health. Or you may want to find a qualified Christian counselor to help you. The person you select will be determined by a number of factors, including their availability and schedule, and your desire. You may want the professional care and confidentiality of a counselor, but be sure that you find one whose counseling is based on biblical principles.

There is a stigma about counseling in the minds of some people. They believe that "all counselors are quacks," and that you have to be "really messed up" to go to one. Not everybody needs to go to a counselor, but many people would benefit from the warmth, affirmation, and objectivity that a good counselor can provide.

The grip of codependency is strong. We cannot make it on our own, so find a friend to help you.

HANDLES ON THE PROCESS

As a codependent learns more about how he has been affected by dysfunctional relationships, he also learns how to respond in new and more positive ways. These new responses are characterized by three essential ingredients: identify, detach, and decide. First he can identify the behaviors, feelings, thoughts, words, and actions that have become the habits of codependency. Then he can detach and reflect about the situation, how he can stop responding in the usual way, and instead respond in a positive, healthy way. After that reflection, he can decide on his course of action. It will be a response based on objective reality, not a reaction based on codependent reflexes.

Identify. Detach. Decide. See it. Analyze it. Choose your response. This is the path to freedom and health.

Let's see how we can identify our codependent behaviors:

• **Identify.** As we learn more about our identity in Christ, and as we see the patterns of codependency in our lives, we will be able to identify many of the specific codependent things we say and do. Also, we'll be able to see some specific characteristics of codependency in others. For some, identifying codependent behavior will be fairly easy: *Oh yeah! I've done that for years!* Others will have a harder time identifying those behaviors. People like this may see a few instances, but they don't see the patterns of codependency very clearly. Still others lack objectivity to such an extent that they don't see any characteristics of their codependency at all. They just don't get the picture, and healing can't begin until the Holy Spirit begins to overcome their denial.

Identifying codependent behavior is the trigger mechanism for objective reflection, and for ultimately living in freedom and godly independence.

Identifying codependent behavior may seem like a very cognitive exercise, but it usually elicits a flood of emotions as we realize how deeply we have been affected. There is both good and bad news in this realization. The good news is: There is hope! The Lord can give us wisdom and strength, and a friend can give us the encouragement we need to fight our battles. The bad news is: What you see is probably only the first layer of the onion. As you deal with the hurts, fears, anger, and habits there, yet another layer will be exposed. Is that discouraging to you? It probably is, but this is reality, and we need to face reality no matter how difficult it is. Remember, you are not alone. The Lord will

give you the grace to endure and progress.
Paul encouraged the believers in Corinth:

> *No temptation has overtaken*
> *you but such as is common to man;*
> *and God is faithful, who will not*
> *allow you to be tempted beyond*
> *what you are able, but with the*
> *temptation will provide the way of*
> *escape also, that you may be able*
> *to endure it.*
>
> 1 Cor. 10:13

The way of escape so that we may endure
begins when we identify our codependent
behavior, then detach and reflect on reality,
and finally, decide on the best course of
action.

• **Detach**. Codependents are trained to
react, not respond. We instinctively rescue,
withdraw, or attack. We feel the compassion
of a rescuer, and we feel anger, hurt, and

self-pity. This instinct is deeply ingrained in us, but we need to change. We need to detach, to separate ourselves from that codependent reaction system, and think, feel, and reflect.

Detachment requires time, objectivity, and distance (emotionally, physically, or both). Circumstances vary so widely that there cannot be a formula for detaching, but there is a question that can help you: *What do I need (time, space, objectivity) so that I can reflect on this situation?*

Sometimes we can identify, detach, and decide in a heartbeat. This is especially true when we've had ample practice in this process. Many times, however, we need to remove ourselves from the offending person or situation to be more objective. The pressure of close proximity is simply too strong. Go to another room, take a drive in the country (under the speed limit!), go away for a weekend. Do whatever you need to do so that you can feel and think. A distraction may help you gain a sense of calm before you reflect. Read a book or magazine, watch a television show, take a walk. Do whatever helps you.

Some psychologists use detach to describe the act of isolating oneself from others in a negative, harmful way. In contrast, codependent literature uses the word to describe a positive, healthy action: stepping back to obtain objectivity about a person or situation. Therefore, detachment is not the same as withdrawal, though it may appear to be at first. Withdrawal is a defensive reaction to block pain and avoid reality. Detachment has the opposite goal: to become objective, deal with reality, feel real emotions, and determine the best course of action.

The Scriptures have a lot to say about reflecting on reality and truth so that we can respond wisely instead of reacting codependently. We are instructed to take time to acquire this wisdom: (see Prov. 4:5-7). A friend sometimes can be instrumental in helping us feel pain and be objective (Prov.

24:3-6). And we can learn how to respond to people who condemn, neglect, and manipulate us (Prov. 26:4-5).

Don't be too discouraged if your first attempts at detaching are painful and awkward. Drastic change takes time, patience, practice, and courage. The more you try to detach, the more confident you will become, and eventually, it will become a very constructive habit for you.

• **Decide**. It is possible to detach, to feel, to think, and to consider your options, but then to be immobilized and not make any decision at all. After we have reflected, we need the courage to act in positive, healthy ways. We need to stop rescuing and controlling, and start saying and doing those things that reflect independence, security, strength, and health. This is extremely important, both for our own sake and for the sake of those we typically rescue and control.

When we detach and become objective, we are able to admit how we feel. We can be angry, sad, glad, or afraid in a safe environment. And we are able to consider our options and make the best choice. Then we can act in confidence.

Making independent choices also means that we can do helpful things for people because we want to, not just because we will feel guilty if we don't.

The key to making sound, independent questions is asking and determining the answer to this crucial question: *Lord, what do You want me to do?* This question usually is confusing for the codependent because he often assumes that the Lord wants him to rescue and control others. He feels guilty if he doesn't do absolutely everything he possibly can for people—and often, he feels guilty even though he does.

Seeking the Lord's direction is still valid for codependents, but our mindsets need to change. That's what detaching is all about.

Don't assume that the Lord always wants you to rescue, help, and/or control people. His primary concern is that we renounce idolatrous behavior in our relationships; that we stop trying to please others in an attempt to gain security and worth from them instead of from Him. When we are independent from the controls of others, then we are open to the Lord's wisdom and direction. Then we can be objective about the question: *Lord, what do You want me to do?*

Codependents normally take responsibility for others but not for themselves. With the Lord's direction and strength, we need to take responsibility for our own lives. If we have been passive, we need to take steps of action. If we have been driven, we need to learn to say no to some things, even if others don't understand or approve. If we have acted like children, we need to start acting like adults.

Take steps to be responsible for your own life and honor the Lord in your personal life, relationships, goals, and habits. Develop a healthy independence from the bondage of pleasing others and a godly dependence on the love, wisdom, and strength of the Lord. This process begins when we ask the crucial question, *Lord, what do You want me to do?*

Identify. Detach. Decide. See it. Analyze it. Choose your response. These ingredients, combined with profound biblical solutions and solid biblical processes, can provide the content and context for God's power to change lives. It may be a long, unpleasant process, but it is the way to health.

Sometimes, as you continue to recognize your propensity to gain a sense of worth by pleasing others, it may seem impossible to change. Hang in there! Objectivity is often painful, but the Lord is a kind and patient Master. He knows your past and He knows your pain. Instead of viewing Him as a demanding God that you can never please, learn to see Him as a kind, gentle Father who will give you all the encouragement, strength, and time you need. Overcoming a lifetime of people-pleasing (idolatry) is hard work, but it is possible. You can be free! As your identity and view of God begin to change, you will have an increasing sense that God does indeed care about you deeply, that He is trustworthy, and that He has a wonderful plan for your life.

Editor's note:

At Rapha, we believe that small groups can provide a nurturing and powerful environment to help people deal with real-life problems such as depression, grief, fear, eating disorders, chemical dependency, codependency, and all kinds of other relational and emotional difficulties. The warmth, honesty, and understanding in those groups helps us understand why we feel and act the way we do. And with the encouragement of others, we can take definitive steps toward healing and health for ourselves and our relationships.

Not all groups, however, provide this kind of "greenhouse" for growth. Some only perpetuate the guilt and loneliness by giving quick and superficial solutions to the deep and often complex problems in our lives.

We urge you to find a group of people in your church, or in a church near you, where the members provide acceptance, love, honesty, and encouragement. Rapha has many different books, workbooks, leader's guides, and types of training so that people in these groups can be nurtured in the love and grace of God and focused on sound biblical principles to help them experience healing and growth.

To obtain a free list of the materials we have available, please write to us at:

> Rapha, Inc.
> 8876 Gulf Freeway, Suite 340
> Houston, TX 77017

NOTES

[1] Adapted from *The Family Trap* by Sharon Wegschieder-Cruse.

[2] Burton White, *The First Three Years of Life*. Rev. Ed. (New York: Prentice-Hall Press, 1985), pp. 323-324.

[3] Melody Beattie, *Codependent No More* (New York: Hazelden Foundation, 1987), p. 31.

[4] Robert S. McGee, Jim Craddock, Pat Springle, *Your Parents and You* (Houston and Dallas, TX: Rapha Publishing/Word, Inc., 1990), p. 3.

[5] Robert S. McGee, *The Search for Significance*. 2nd ed. (Houston and Dallas, TX: Rapha Publishing/Word, Inc., 1990), pp. 55-60.

ABOUT THE AUTHOR...

Pat Springle is the senior vice president of Rapha Resources. He served on the staff of Campus Crusade for Christ for 18 years, 11 years as their Texas area director. Pat lives in Houston with his wife, Joyce, and his two children, Catherine and Taylor. He is the author of *Making Choices That Honor God*, *Rapha's 12-Step Program for Overcoming Codependency*, and *Close Enough to Care*, and co-author of *Your Parents and You*, *Rapha's 12-Step Program for Overcoming Chemical Dependency*, *Getting Unstuck*, and *Rapha's Handbook for Group Leaders*.